Getting Around

Sally Odgers

Illustrated by Virginia Barrett

Some people get around on their feet.

They walk or run.

They jump or skip or even hop.

Some people get around in water.

They swim or paddle.

They row boats or float in rubber rings.

Some people get around on wheels.

They roller-skate or ride bikes.

They ride in wheelchairs or travel in strollers.

Some people get around in unusual ways.
They walk on stilts or walk on their hands.
They ride unicycles.

Some people get around by riding on animals.

They ride horses or donkeys.

They ride camels or elephants.

Some people get around by sliding.
They use sleds or skis on snow.
They use skates on ice.

Some people get around by using engines.

They drive cars or trucks.

They ride in motorboats or on motorbikes.

Some people get around by using public transportation.

They ride on buses or catch trains.

They ride on ferries or on subways.

Some people get around by flying through the air.
They ride in balloons or fly in planes.
They fly hang gliders or ride in helicopters.

11

When you were small, you got around by crawling.
How do you get around today?
Do you walk and jump and hop?
Do you swim and roll and ride?
How do you get around?